Dream Big, Start Small: A Kid's Guide to Entrepreneurship

New York City Books
www.nycitybooks.com

217 Peace Pipe Way
Georgetown TX 78628 USA

Printed in the United States of America

Publisher's Cataloging-in-Publication data
Arat, Mel
Dream Big, Start Small: A Kid's Guide to Entrepreneurship

LCCN: 2023907983

Amazon Print ISBN- 9798393460075

Dream Big,
Start Small:
A Kid's Guide to
Entrepreneurship

Mel ARAT

New York City Books

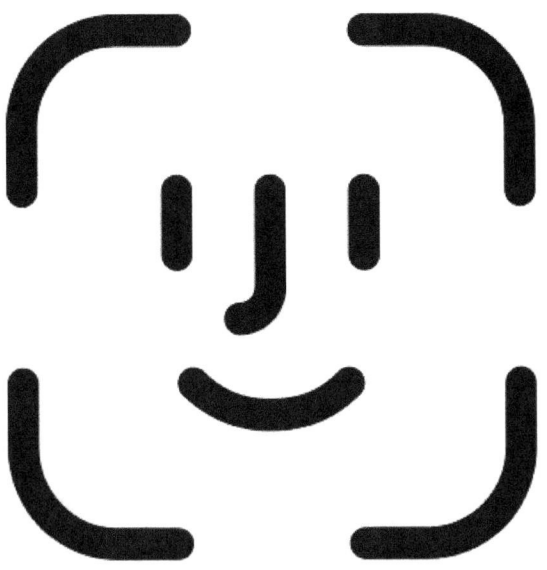

Preface

Welcome to **Dream Big, Start Small: A Kid's Guide to Entrepreneurship!** This book is all about helping kids like you turn their big dreams into reality by starting their own businesses.

Starting a business may seem like something only grown-ups can do, but the truth is that anyone can become an entrepreneur - even kids! With a little creativity, hard work, and determination, you can create a successful and profitable business that makes a positive impact on the world around you.

In this book, you'll learn about all the different aspects of starting a business, from finding your passion and generating ideas, to making a plan, pricing your products or services, and expanding your reach. You'll also learn how to handle challenges, stay motivated when things get tough, and keep improving what you offer.

My hope is that this book will inspire you to dream big and take action to make those dreams a reality. We believe that entrepreneurship is a powerful way for kids to develop important skills like creativity, problem-solving, and leadership, while also making a positive impact on their communities and the world.

So, whether you want to start a lemonade stand, sell handmade crafts, or create the next big tech startup, this book is for you. Dream big, start small, and let's create a world where anyone can be an entrepreneur, no matter their age!

Table of Contents

Introduction

Are you ready to learn how to turn your passions into a successful business venture? In this book, we'll explore the journeys of young entrepreneurs who turned their ideas into thriving companies, and I'll show you how you can do it too!

In chapter one, we will discover what it means to be an entrepreneur and why it's cool to start a business like Christian Owens did. In chapter two, we will explore how to find our passions and make a difference like Ashley Qualls. Chapter three will be all about idea generation and turning our ideas into something real like Cameron Johnson. In chapter four, we will learn how to plan our business, identify our customers, and set goals like John Koon. Then in chapter five, we will spread the word about our business and get people excited like Evan. In chapter six, we will explore how to make money by pricing our products or services and ensuring that we make more than we spend like Farrhad Acidwalla. In chapter seven, we will learn how to grow our business by improving what we offer like Adam Horwitz. Finally, in chapter eight, we will learn how to handle challenges and keep going when things get tough like Maddie Bradshaw. So get ready to explore the world of entrepreneurship and become a successful business owner!

Chapter 1: Let's start a business!

Let's start a business! But first, what exactly is a business? A business is something that sells products or services to people who need or want them. And guess what? You can start a business too!

First, think about what you're really good at. Do you love baking cookies or cupcakes? Are you great at making jewelry or drawing cool pictures? Maybe you love taking care of pets or making people laugh. Whatever it is that you love doing, there's probably a way to turn it into a business.

Next, think about what problems you can solve. Maybe your neighborhood needs a dog-walking service, or your school needs healthy snacks for kids. Or maybe you can create a fun game or activity that people will love. The possibilities are endless!

Once you have an idea for your business, it's time to make a plan. This means figuring out how much money you'll need, who your customers will be, and how you'll get the word out about your business. It might seem like a lot of work, but don't worry - we'll go through all the steps together.

Starting a business is a big adventure, and it can be a little scary at times. But with the right attitude and some hard work, you can make your business a success. And who knows - maybe someday you'll be the next big entrepreneur, inspiring others to follow their dreams too!

What does it mean to be an entrepreneur?

Simply put, it means you start your own business and come up with cool ideas for products or services that people want or need. It's like being a problem-solver or a creator!

Entrepreneurs are people who love to think outside the box and try new things. They aren't afraid to take risks and make mistakes, because they know that's how they learn and grow. And even when things get tough, entrepreneurs keep going and find ways to overcome obstacles.

Being an entrepreneur is about using your skills and passions to make a difference in the world. You might create a new toy that kids love to play with, or invent a tool that makes life easier for grown-ups. You might even start a business that helps your community in some way, like a recycling program or a charity event.

But being an entrepreneur is also about having fun! When you start your own business, you get to be your own boss and make all the decisions. You get to be creative and come up with new ideas. And best of all, you get to share your talents and make a positive impact on the world around you.

Why is it cool to be an entrepreneur?

Well, for starters, you get to be your own boss and make all the decisions. That means you get to be in charge of what you create, how you create it, and who you sell it to. It's like being the captain of your own ship!

Being an entrepreneur is also cool because you get to be creative and use your imagination. You can come up with new and exciting ideas that no one else has thought of before. You can invent something that helps people, or create a game that everyone loves to play. The possibilities are endless!

Another cool thing about being an entrepreneur is that you get to learn lots of new things. You'll learn about marketing, sales, budgeting, and more. And even if your first business doesn't work out, you'll learn from your mistakes and be better prepared for your next adventure.

Finally, being an entrepreneur is cool because you get to make a difference in the world. You might create a product that makes people happy, or provide a service that helps your community. You might even inspire others to follow their dreams and start their own businesses. When you're an entrepreneur, you have the power to change the world for the better.

Case Study: Christian Owens

Christian Owens, a young and innovative entrepreneur, started his own company, Macbundlebox, at just 16 years old. His subscription service offered discounted bundles of Mac applications, inspired by his own experience of needing software for hbis web design business. Owens identified a gap in the market and capitalized on it, showcasing the importance of paying attention to the needs of potential customers.

Despite challenges such as licensing agreements and new competitors, Owens remained resilient and continued to innovate, adapting his business model to stay ahead. He demonstrated the importance of remaining flexible and open to change, an essential lesson for all entrepreneurs.

Owens' success led him to be recognized by top media outlets, such as the BBC and TechCrunch, and his business achievements inspired many young entrepreneurs to follow their passions. His story is a testament to the fact that age is just a number and anyone can achieve success if they have the drive and determination to pursue their goals.

Business lessons from Christian Owens' story:

1. **Identify a gap in the market:** Owens identified a need for discounted bundles of Mac applications and created Macbundlebox to cater to this need. Aspiring entrepreneurs can learn from this lesson and identify a gap in the market that they can address with their own products or services.

2. **Adapt to change:** Owens faced challenges such as licensing agreements and new competitors, but he remained resilient and continued to adapt his business model to stay ahead. Entrepreneurs should be flexible and open to change to stay competitive.

3. **Pay attention to customer needs:** Owens' idea for Macbundlebox was inspired by his own experience of needing software for his web design business. He identified a common problem and created a solution that addressed the needs of his target audience. Entrepreneurs should pay attention to the needs and desires of their potential customers to create products and services that are in high demand.

4. **Pursue your passions: Owens** was passionate about web design and saw an opportunity to create a business in this field. Entrepreneurs should pursue their passions and create businesses that align with their interests and strengths.

5. **Age is just a number:** Owens started Macbundlebox at the young age of 16, demonstrating that anyone can achieve success regardless of their age.

Design a Logo for Your Business:

Introduction: In this exercise you will develop a graphic sign for your business.

Materials:
- Paper, Pencil, pen, or markers
- Optional: computer and design software (if available)

Instructions:
1. Think of a business idea or use an existing one. It can be anything from a bakery to a sports team to a clothing brand.
2. Write down the name of the business.
3. Brainstorm some ideas for what the logo could look like. What colors do you want to use? What symbols or images could represent the business?
4. Sketch some rough ideas for the logo on paper.
5. Pick your favorite sketch and start refining it. Add more details and clean up the lines.
6. Decide on the final colors and finish your logo.
7. Present your logo to others and explain why you chose certain elements.

Tips:

- Keep it simple. A good logo should be easily recognizable and memorable.
- Use contrasting colors that stand out.
- Make sure the logo reflects the business or product it represents.
- Think about where the logo will be used, such as on a website, business card, or t-shirt.

Chapter 2: Finding your passion

Finding your passion is all about figuring out what you love to do! Do you have a hobby that you could do for hours and never get bored? Do you have a talent that makes you feel proud and accomplished? That could be your passion!

Think about the things that make you happiest and most excited. Maybe you love to draw, dance, or sing. Maybe you love to play sports or cook yummy food. Whatever it is that makes you feel good, that's probably where your passion lies.

Once you've figured out what your passion is, it's time to think about how you can use it to help others. Maybe you can create a business that provides a service or product that people need or want. For example, if you love baking, you could start a cupcake business and make people's birthdays even more special.

Or maybe you can use your passion to solve a problem in your community. If you love animals, you could start a pet-sitting or dog-walking business. If you love the environment, you could start a recycling program or create eco-friendly products.
When you're doing something you're passionate about, it won't feel like work at all. And who knows - maybe your passion will turn into your dream job!

What are you good at?

Everyone has something they're good at - it could be drawing, playing sports, making people laugh, or even organizing things. Think about the things that you do well and that come naturally to you.

When you're good at something, it usually means you enjoy doing it too. You might feel proud of yourself when you do it, or you might just love the feeling of being in the zone and doing something you're good at.

Once you've figured out what you're good at, it's time to think about how you can use that skill to make a business. For example, if you're good at baking, you could start a cookie or cupcake business. If you're good at playing guitar, you could give music lessons or play at parties. The key is to find a way to use your skill in a way that helps others. When you're doing something you're good at, it usually means you're making a positive impact on the world. And when you're making a positive impact, people will want to support your business and help you succeed!

Know Yourself

1. What are some activities that you enjoy doing and seem to come naturally to you?
2. Can you think of a time when you accomplished something that you felt proud of? What skills did you use to accomplish that task?
3. What are some things that your friends or family members have complimented you on? Are there any skills or talents that they have noticed that you possess?

What do you love doing?

This is all about thinking about the things that make you happiest and bring you the most joy. Maybe it's playing with your favorite toys, dancing to your favorite music, or even just spending time with your family and friends.

When you love doing something, it usually means you're good at it too. You might feel like you could do it for hours and never get bored. And when you're doing something, you love, it usually means you're making a positive impact on the world in some way.

Once you've figured out what you love doing, it's time to think about how you can turn that into a business. Maybe you can create a product or service that helps others enjoy what you love doing too. For example, if you love making crafts, you could create a business that sells your crafts or teaches others how to make them.

Or maybe you can use what you love doing to solve a problem in your community. For example, if you love playing sports, you could start a sports program for kids in your neighborhood who don't have access to sports equipment or facilities.
And when you're making a positive impact, people will want to support your business and help you succeed!

Self-Discovery

1. What are some activities that you would do even if you weren't getting paid for them?
2. What hobbies or interests do you have that you could turn into a business or career?
3. If you had a free day with no responsibilities, how would you choose to spend your time?

How can you make a difference?

How can you make a difference with your skills and interests? It's all about thinking about how you can use your talents to help others and make the world a better place. When you're doing something you love and you're good at, it usually means you're making a positive impact in some way.

For example, if you're good at playing an instrument, you could share your love of music with others by giving lessons or playing at events. If you love baking, you could make people happy by creating yummy treats for them to enjoy. And if you're great at organizing things, you could help make your community a better place by organizing a charity event or clean-up day.

The key is to find a way to use your skills and interests to solve a problem or meet a need. When you're doing something that helps others, it usually means you're making a positive impact on the world. And when you're making a positive impact, people will want to support your business and help you succeed!

So, think about how you can make a difference with your skills and interests. What problems can you solve? What needs can you meet? And how can you do it in a way that's exciting for you? When you find the answers to these questions, you'll be well on your way to becoming an awesome entrepreneur!

What change do you want to create?

1. What are some issues that you care about? How could you use your skills and talents to make a positive difference in those areas?
2. Can you think of a time when you helped someone or made a positive impact on someone's life? How did it make you feel, and could you do something similar on a larger scale?
3. How could you use your business or career to make a positive impact on your community or the world?

Case Study: Ashley Qualls

Ashley Qualls is a young entrepreneur who started Whateverlife.com, a website that provides free Myspace layouts and tutorials on how to customize Myspace profiles, when she was just 14 years old. The idea for the website came to her when she was looking for a way to create a unique Myspace profile for herself without having to spend any money. She realized that other teenagers might be in the same situation, so she decided to start a website that would offer free Myspace layouts and other resources to help young people customize their profiles.

The website quickly gained popularity, and within a few years, Whateverlife.com was attracting millions of visitors each month. Qualls was featured in several media outlets, including The New York Times and Forbes, and was even offered $1.5 million for the website, which she turned down.

Despite the success of Whateverlife.com, Qualls faced some challenges along the way, including legal battles with Myspace over the use of copyrighted images in her layouts. She also had to navigate the world of online advertising, which was relatively new at the time.

Today, Qualls is no longer involved with Whateverlife.com, but the website still exists as a testament to her entrepreneurial spirit and creativity.

Business lessons from Ashley Qualls' story:

1. **Find a niche:** Ashley Qualls identified a gap in the market for Myspace layouts and tutorials that catered to a younger demographic. She capitalized on this opportunity by creating Whateverlife.com. Entrepreneurs should identify a specific niche or target audience to serve, as it can help differentiate their business from competitors.

2. **Be resourceful:** Qualls started Whateverlife.com with no outside funding, using her own computer and software to create the website. Entrepreneurs should be resourceful and make the most of what they have available to them.

3. **Focus on quality:** Qualls' success was due in part to the high-quality designs and content she provided on Whateverlife.com. Entrepreneurs should focus on providing quality products or services to their customers in order to build a loyal customer base.

4. Learn from mistakes: Qualls faced legal battles over the use of copyrighted images on her website. She learned from these mistakes and used original artwork moving forward. Entrepreneurs should be open to learning from their mistakes and make necessary changes to improve their businesses.

5. **Stay motivated:** Qualls continued to work hard and remain motivated despite facing challenges and criticism. Entrepreneurs should stay focused on their goals and remain motivated to overcome obstacles and achieve success.

"Passion Quest"

Introduction: This exercise aims helping you explore your interests and identify your passion.

Materials: Pen/pencil, paper

Instructions:

1. Begin by writing down a list of your favorite activities and hobbies.
2. Next, think about what you enjoy about each of these activities. Write down a brief description of what you love about each one.
3. Consider your strengths and talents. What are you good at? Write down a list of things you are confident in doing.
4. Think about what you want to learn or try in the future. Write down a list of new experiences you would like to have.
5. Look for patterns or themes in your lists. Do you notice any common interests or passions that you could pursue further?
6. Create a mind map or drawing that visually represents your passions and interests. Use different colors and shapes to organize your ideas.
7. Finally, write a short paragraph describing your passion(s) and how you plan to pursue them. Think about ways you can incorporate your passions into your daily life or future career goals.
8. Share your mind map and paragraph with a friend or classmate. Discuss your passions and how you can support each other in pursuing them.

Chapter 3 Idea Generation

Idea generation is all about coming up with cool ideas for your business! This is one of the best parts, where you get to use your creativity and imagination to think of new and exciting ways to make a difference in the world.

To get started, think about the problems you see in your community or the things that you think could be better. Maybe you notice that there aren't enough healthy snacks for kids at your school, or that there aren't enough activities for kids to do outside. These are opportunities for you to come up with a business idea that solves these problems!

Next, think about the things that you love doing or are really good at. Maybe you love baking or making crafts, or maybe you're great at organizing things. These skills can be the basis for a business idea too!

Once you have a few ideas in mind, it's time to evaluate them and see which ones have the most potential. Think about things like how much money it would cost to start the business, how many people would want to buy your product or service, and how you can stand out from the competition.

The most important thing is not be afraid to take risks! You might come up with an idea that doesn't work out, but that's okay - it's all part of the process. Keep trying and keep coming up with new ideas until you find one that's a perfect fit for you and your goals.

Let's brainstorm!

This is where we get to use our imaginations and come up with lots of cool ideas for our business. The goal is to think of as many ideas as possible, even if they seem silly or impossible at first.

To get started, remember the things that you love doing and the things that you're good at. What problems do you see in your community or in the world that you could solve with your skills and interests?

Next, think about the things that other people need or want. Maybe you've noticed that your friends and family are always looking for a certain product or service, or maybe you've seen a need in your community that you could fill.

Now it's time to get creative! Think about all the different ways you could solve these problems or meet these needs. Write down every idea that comes to mind, no matter how crazy it might seem.

Once you have a long list of ideas, it's time to start evaluating them. Think about things like how much money it would cost to start the business, how many people would want to buy your product or service, and how you can stand out from the competition.

You might come up with an idea that doesn't work out, but that's okay - it's all part of the process. Keep brainstorming and keep coming up with new ideas until you find one that's a perfect fit for you and your goals.

Running a brainstorm is an exciting way to come up with lots of ideas. Here are the steps to run a brainstorm:

1. **Gather your team:** Gather a group of people that you want to brainstorm with. This could be your friends, family members, or classmates.
2. **Define the problem:** Start by defining the problem or challenge that you want to brainstorm about. Make sure everyone understands the problem and agrees on what you're trying to solve.
3. **Set the rules:** Set some rules for the brainstorm. For example, everyone should be respectful of each other's ideas, and there should be no criticizing or judging. Encourage everyone to be creative and open-minded.
4. **Start the brainstorm:** Start by asking everyone to share their ideas. Encourage everyone to speak up, and write down every idea that is shared. Don't worry about whether the ideas are good or bad - just write them down.
5. **Build on each other's ideas:** Once everyone has shared their ideas, start building on each other's ideas. See if there are any ideas that can be combined or improved upon.
6. **Choose the best ideas:** Once you have a lot of ideas, start to choose the best ones. Look for ideas that are practical, creative, and fit with your goals.
7. **Take action:** Finally, take action on the ideas that you've chosen. Put them into practice and see how they work. Remember, it's okay if not all of your ideas work out - that's all part of the brainstorming process!

How can we solve problems in our community?

This is a great question to ask yourself when you're brainstorming ideas for your business. When you solve a problem, you're making a positive impact on the world around you.

To get started, think about the problems you see in your community. Maybe there's a park that needs cleaning up, or there's a shortage of healthy food options in your neighborhood. These are opportunities for you to use your skills and talents to make a difference!

Next, think about the things that you love doing or are really good at. Maybe you love baking or making crafts, or maybe you're great at organizing things. These skills can be the basis for a business idea that solves a problem in your community.

Once you have an idea in mind, it's time to start planning. Think about how you can make your business idea a reality. Who will your customers be? How will you get the word out about your business? What supplies or equipment will you need?

Remember, the key to solving problems in your community is to be creative! When you're doing something you love, it won't feel like work at all. And when you're making a positive impact, people will want to support your business and help you succeed!

Solve Problems:

1. What are some problems that you see in your community that you would like to help solve?
2. How can you use your skills and talents to make a positive impact in your community?
3. Who are some people or organizations in your community that you could work with to solve problems?

How can we turn our ideas into something real?

This is where we start to bring our ideas to life and turn them into a real business. It might seem a little scary at first, but with some planning and hard work, you can make it happen!

First, it's important to create a plan. This means thinking about all the things you'll need to make your idea a reality. What supplies or equipment will you need? Who will your customers be? How will you get the word out about your business?

Next, you'll need to start taking action! This might mean buying supplies, designing a logo, or creating a website. You might also need to start practicing your skills and perfecting your product or service.

Remember, starting a business takes time and effort, so don't be afraid to ask for help! Talk to your parents, teachers, or other adults in your community who might be able to offer advice or support.

Keep learning and growing, and never give up on your dreams. When you turn your ideas into something real, you're making a positive impact on the world around you and showing others that anything is possible!

Questions

1. What are some steps that you need to take to turn your ideas into a real project or business?
2. How can you break down your big ideas into smaller, more manageable steps?
3. Who are some people or resources that you could reach out to for help in turning your ideas into something real?

Ideas in Action: Generating Ideas

In this section, which I call "Ideas in Action," we will explore how theories can be put into practice by using the classic example of a lemonade stand business. Let's try to generate ideas to create a different type of lemonade stand.

Generate Ideas for a Better Lemonade Stand Business

Looking for ways to make your lemonade stand business more exciting and profitable? By adding some unique twists to your traditional lemonade recipe, you can attract more customers and stand out from your competition. Here are some fun and creative ideas to spice up your lemonade stand and make it the talk of the town.

- Offer different types of lemonade flavors, such as strawberry, blueberry, or raspberry lemonade.
- Sell snacks to go with the lemonade, such as cookies or popcorn.
- Add a DIY lemonade station, where customers can mix and match their own flavors.
- Provide free samples to customers who make a purchase.
- Create a loyalty program where customers can earn a free lemonade after purchasing a certain number.

Case Study: Cameron Johnson

Cameron Johnson is an American entrepreneur who became a millionaire before the age of 21. He started his first business, a greeting card company called Cheers and Tears, when he was just 9 years old.

Johnson's company quickly gained popularity, and he began selling his cards at local stores and malls. By the age of 12, he had expanded his business to include online sales, and he was making thousands of dollars per month. Inspired by his early success, Johnson went on to start several other successful ventures, including an online advertising company and a mobile app development company. He also wrote a book called "You Call the Shots", which detailed his journey as a young entrepreneur and offered advice to other aspiring business owners.

In addition to his entrepreneurial endeavors, Johnson is also a philanthropist. He has donated millions of dollars to various causes, including education and healthcare initiatives.

Business lessons from Cameron Johnson's story:

Start small and grow: Cameron Johnson started with a small greeting card business, Cheers and Tears, and then expanded to other ventures. Entrepreneurs should consider starting small and then gradually expanding their business as they gain experience and resources.

Network and build relationships: Johnson built strong relationships with suppliers, customers, and investors, which helped him grow his businesses. Entrepreneurs should focus on building strong relationships with stakeholders to help support their growth.

Adapt to new technologies: Johnson adapted to new technologies such as the internet, using it to market and sell his products. Entrepreneurs should stay up-to-date with new technologies and use them to their advantage in their business.

Take calculated risks: Johnson took calculated risks in his business, such as investing in new ventures and expanding to new markets. Entrepreneurs should be willing to take risks in their business, but also evaluate the potential risks and rewards before making a decision.

Embrace failure: Johnson experienced failures in his business, such as with his mobile app development company. However, he learned from these failures and used them to improve his future businesses. Entrepreneurs should embrace failure as a learning opportunity and use it to improve their future endeavors.

Exercise: "Pick a Business Idea"

This is an activity you can do on your own to come up with a business idea that you think would be fun and successful.

Here are the steps:

1. Brainstorm: First, take a few minutes to brainstorm some things you are good at or enjoy doing. Maybe you're good at baking, or love playing video games, or enjoy playing with pets. Write down a list of your skills and interests.

2. Identify a problem: Think about problems that you or others face in your community or in your daily life. This could be something as simple as not having enough snacks available at school, or something more complex like a lack of accessible parks in your neighborhood. Write down a list of these problems.

3. Connect skills and problems: Take a look at your list of skills and interests, and try to match them with the problems you identified. For example, if you love baking and noticed a lack of healthy snack options at school, maybe you could start a business selling healthy baked goods to your classmates.

4. Research: Once you have a few ideas for businesses, do some research to see if they are feasible. Look at other similar businesses in your area, and see if there is a demand for your product or service. Think about how much money you might need to start the business, and how you could get that money.

5. Choose your idea: After researching, pick one business idea that you think would be the most fun and successful. Write down a brief description of your idea, including what problem it solves and how it will make money.

That's it! This exercise should take about an hour to complete. Good luck, and have fun coming up with your own business idea!

Chapter 4: Business planning

Business planning is all about creating a roadmap for your business. It's like making a plan for a big trip - you need to think about where you're going, how you'll get there, and what you'll need along the way.

Planning is an important step in starting a business, and it's always better to have some help. Whether it's a friend, family member, or even a teacher, it's always good to have someone to bounce ideas off of and help you stay organized.

To get started, sit down with your helper and think about your goals. What do you want to achieve with your business? Do you want to make a certain amount of money, help a certain number of people, or create a certain number of products or services?

Next, think about your customers. Who are they? What do they need or want? How can you make their lives better with your product or service?

Once you have a good understanding of your goals and your customers, it's time to start thinking about the logistics. This means things like how much money it will cost to start your business, what supplies or equipment you'll need, and how you'll market your product or service.

Make sure to write down your ideas and plans on paper or on a computer. This will help you stay organized and make changes as needed. And don't forget to set deadlines and goals for yourself to help you stay on track.

Who are our customers?

Customers are the people who will buy your product or service. It's important to think about who your customers are so that you can create a product or service that meets their needs and wants.

To start, think about the problem you're trying to solve with your business. Who is affected by this problem? Who needs or wants a solution?

Next, think about the people in your community who might be interested in your product or service. Are they kids, adults, or both? What are their interests, hobbies, and needs?

Once you have a good understanding of who your customers are, it's time to start thinking about how you can reach them. This means things like creating marketing materials, reaching out to potential customers, and making sure your product or service is easily accessible to them.

Remember, it's important to listen to your customers and take their feedback into account. This will help you create a product or service that they'll love and want to buy again and again.

Building a business is an exciting adventure, and it's always more exciting when you have happy customers who love what you're doing.

Who is your customer?

1. Who is affected by the problem you're trying to solve with your business?
2. Who might be interested in your product or service, and what are their interests and needs?
3. How can you reach your potential customers through marketing and accessibility?

How much money do we need to start?

Starting a business can cost money, but it doesn't have to be expensive. It's important to create a budget and figure out how much money you'll need to start your business.

To get started, think about what you'll need to buy to get your business up and running. This might include supplies, equipment, and marketing materials.

Next, do some research to figure out how much these things will cost. Look online, visit stores, and talk to other business owners to get an idea of how much things cost.

Once you have a good idea of how much things will cost, it's time to create a budget. This means thinking about how much money you have to start your business and how much you'll need to spend on each item.

Remember, it's important to be realistic with your budget. Starting a business takes time and effort, and it's important to have enough money to cover your expenses.

If you don't have enough money to start your business, don't worry! There are lots of ways to raise money, like doing a fundraiser or getting a loan from a bank or family member.

And don't forget, you can always start small and grow your business over time. The most important thing is to get started!

What do you need?

1. What do you need to buy to start your business, like supplies and equipment?
2. How can you find out how much these things will cost?
3. How can you create a budget for your business, considering how much money you have to start and how much you'll need to spend on each item?

How much do we want to make?

Making money is one of the goals of starting a business, but it's important to have a realistic idea of how much you want to make.

To start, think about how much money you need to cover your expenses and make a profit. This means thinking about things like the cost of supplies, equipment, and marketing materials, as well as any fees or taxes you'll need to pay.

Next, think about how much you want to make in a certain amount of time. Do you want to make a certain amount of money per month, per year, or over the lifetime of your business?

Once you have a clear idea of how much you want to make, it's time to start taking action! Create a budget and a pricing strategy to help you achieve your financial goals. Remember, making money is important, but it's not the only goal of starting a business. It's also important to create a product or service that makes a positive impact on the world around you and helps improve the lives of others.

And don't forget, starting a business takes time and effort. It's important to have patience and be willing to make changes as needed to achieve your financial goals.

How much do you need to start?

1. How much money do you need to cover expenses and make a profit?
2. How can you calculate the cost of supplies, equipment, marketing materials, and fees or taxes?
3. How much money do you want to make in a certain amount of time, like per month, per year, or over the lifetime of your business?

Ideas in Action: Business Plan for the Lemonade Stand

In this section, which I call "Ideas in Action," we will explore how theories can be put into practice by using the classic example of a lemonade stand business.

Product: Our lemonade stand will sell delicious homemade lemonade made from fresh lemons, sugar, and water.

Customers: Our lemonade stand will target people of all ages who are thirsty and looking for a refreshing drink on a hot day.

Costs and Income: We will purchase lemons, sugar, and cups for our lemonade stand. We will sell each cup of lemonade for $1. We estimate that we can sell 50 cups of lemonade, resulting in $50 in revenue. After deducting the cost of lemons, sugar, and cups, we estimate a profit of $25.

Strategy: We will set up our lemonade stand in a busy park or near a busy street to attract customers. We will make sure to have a catchy sign that will attract people's attention. We will also offer free samples to attract more customers. Additionally, we will provide great customer service to make sure that our customers keep coming back to our lemonade stand.

Case Study: John Koon

John Koon is a Chinese-American entrepreneur who started Extreme Performance Motorsports (EPMS), a company that specialized in customizing high-end cars for wealthy clients.

Koon grew up in New York City and developed a passion for cars at a young age. He started his career in the automotive industry by working as a mechanic, but he soon realized that he wanted to do more than just fix cars - he wanted to create something truly unique.

In 2003, Koon founded EPMS with the goal of providing customized cars that were not only visually stunning, but also performed at the highest level. His company quickly gained a reputation for producing some of the most powerful and high-performing cars on the market, and he began attracting wealthy clients from around the world.

EPMS's success was not without its challenges, however. Koon faced legal troubles over allegations of fraud and embezzlement, which eventually led to his arrest and imprisonment. Despite these setbacks, EPMS continued to operate under new ownership, and Koon remains a respected figure in the automotive industry.

Today, Koon is known not only for his business acumen but also for his philanthropy. He has donated millions of dollars to various causes, including education and healthcare initiatives in China.

Business lessons from John Koon's story:

Identify your passion: John Koon had a passion for cars, which led him to start his own auto parts business at just 16 years old. Entrepreneurs should identify their own passions and consider starting a business that aligns with their interests.

Seize opportunities: Koon saw an opportunity to start the first auto parts business in New York City and seized the opportunity. Entrepreneurs should keep their eyes open for potential business opportunities and be willing to take risks.

Build relationships: Koon built strong relationships with customers and suppliers, which helped him grow his business. Entrepreneurs should focus on building strong relationships with stakeholders such as customers, suppliers, and employees.

Focus on quality: Koon's company, Extreme Performance Motorsports, focused on customizing high-end cars to meet the specific needs of customers. Entrepreneurs should focus on providing high-quality products or services to their customers in order to build a loyal customer base.

Overcome challenges: Koon faced legal troubles and setbacks in his business, but he remained determined and continued to build his businesses. Entrepreneurs should be resilient and overcome challenges in order to achieve success.

Exercise: Paving the Way to Your Dream Business

This exercise, titled "Paving the Way to Your Dream Business," provides a step-by-step guide for you to create a business plan, including choosing a product or service, identifying target customers, setting goals, planning a budget, and creating an action plan.

1. **Choose a business idea:** Think of a product or service that you would like to offer. It can be something you're passionate about or something you think people need.
2. **Identify your target customers:** Who are the people that would be interested in your product or service? What are their needs and preferences? How can you reach them?
3. **Set goals:** What do you want to achieve with your business? Set realistic and specific goals, such as the amount of money you want to make or the number of customers you want to reach.
4. **Plan your budget:** How much money do you need to start your business? What are the expenses you need to cover, such as supplies, marketing, and rent? Create a budget plan that outlines your estimated income and expenses.
5. **Create an action plan:** How are you going to make your business a reality? List the steps you need to take to start and grow your business, such as registering your business name, creating a website, and networking with potential customers. Set deadlines for each step to keep yourself accountable.

Chapter 5: Let's Spread the Word

Telling people about our business is an important part of getting the word out and attracting customers. But it can be a little scary at first! Here are some tips to help you get started:

1. **Start with your friends and family.** They're already familiar with you and your interests, and they'll be excited to support your new business.
2. **Use social media.** Social media is a great way to reach a lot of people quickly and easily. Create a page or profile for your business and start sharing updates, photos, and information about your products or services.
3. **Participate in community events.** Look for opportunities to participate in local events, like fairs, festivals, or farmers' markets. This is a great way to get your business in front of a lot of people and make connections in your community.
4. **Offer discounts or incentives.** People love a good deal! Offer a discount or special incentive to people who try your product or service for the first time.

Telling people about your business is all about building relationships and creating connections. Be friendly, approachable, and excited about what you're doing, and people will be more likely to support you and spread the word about your business.

Starting a business is an adventure, and it's always more enjoyable when you're sharing it with others.

Word-of-Mouth-Marketing

1. Who are some people that you can tell about your business first, like friends and family?
2. How can you use social media to reach a lot of people quickly and easily?
3. What are some community events that you could participate in to promote your business?
4. How could you offer a discount or special incentive to people who try your product or service for the first time?

How can we get people excited about our business?

Getting people excited about your business is all about building relationships and creating connections. Here are some ways to get people excited about what you're doing:

1. **Show your enthusiasm.** When you're excited about your business, it will show! Be passionate and energetic when you talk about your product or service, and people will be more likely to get excited too.

2. **Offer a unique experience. Think** about what makes your business different from others, and highlight those unique qualities. Whether it's a interesting and creative product, excellent customer service, or a one-of-a-kind experience, find ways to stand out and make a lasting impression on your customers.

3. **Give back to your community.** People love to support businesses that are doing good in their community. Look for ways to give back, whether it's through donations to a local charity, participating in community events, or volunteering your time and talents.

4. **Create a buzz.** Use printed and digital media and other marketing strategies to create buzz and excitement around your business. Offer special promotions, giveaways, or sneak peeks of new products or services to keep your customers engaged and excited.

When people see that you're doing something you love and sharing it, they will naturally be drawn to your business and want to support you.

Engaging with people
1. How can you show your enthusiasm and passion for your business when you talk to others about it?
2. What makes your business unique, and how can you highlight those qualities to stand out from others?
3. How can you give back to your community through your business, such as by donating to charity or volunteering your time?
4. What are some ways you can create excitement and buzz around your business, like offering special promotions or sneak peeks of new products or services?

How can we show them what we have to offer?

Showing people what you have to offer is an important part of running a successful business. Here are some easy ways to showcase your products or services:

1. **Create eye-catching displays.** Use colorful and creative displays to showcase your products or services. This can be as simple as setting up a table with samples, or as elaborate as creating a full storefront display.
2. **Offer demos or free samples.** People love to try before they buy! Offer free demos or samples of your product or service to give people a taste of what you have to offer.
3. **Use Various Platforms on Internet.** Internet is a great way to showcase your products or services. Use high-quality photos and videos to showcase your products, and share updates and special offers with your followers.
4. **Create a website.** A website is a great way to showcase your business and make it easy for people to learn more about what you have to offer. Make sure your website is easy to navigate and includes all the information people need to make a purchase.

Your excitement about your product or service, it will show, and people will be more likely to want to try it out for themselves.

Showcase Your Products

1. How can you use creative and colorful displays to showcase your products or services?
2. Why do people like demos or free samples, and how can you offer them to potential customers?
3. How can you use internet to showcase your products or services and share updates and special offers with your followers?
4. What are some important things to include on your website, like easy navigation, customer reviews, and all the information people need to make a purchase?

Ideas in Action: Word of Mouth Marketing

Now it's time to see how you can use the word-of-mouth-marketing for your lemonade stand.

Step 1: Get the word out

- Tell your family and friends about your lemonade stand and ask them to spread the word to their friends.
- Create flyers and posters to hang up around your neighborhood and local community bulletin boards.

Step 2: Be Social on Social Media

- Use social media platforms like Instagram and Facebook to share pictures of your lemonade stand and post updates about any specials or promotions you might be running.
- Use hashtags like #lemonadestand or #refreshingtreats to help your posts get seen by a wider audience.

Step 3: Customer Feedback and Engagement

- Ask your customers for feedback and make changes based on their suggestions. For example, if a customer suggests adding a new flavor, consider trying it out.
- Respond to any comments or messages you receive on your social media accounts to keep your customers engaged.

Step 4: Incentivize Customer Referrals

- Offer a discount or free lemonade to customers who refer their friends to your stand.
- Provide customers with business cards or flyers they can share with their friends to help spread the word.

Case Study: Evan

Evan is a young boy who, with the help of his father, started a YouTube channel called EvanTubeHD. The channel features Evan unboxing and reviewing toys and games, and quickly gained a large following of kids and parents alike.

Evan's father, Jared, initially started the channel as a way to bond with his son and share their hobby with others. However, as the channel's popularity grew, they began to monetize their content through advertising and sponsorships.

In addition to EvanTubeHD, the family also started a second channel called EvanTubeRAW, which features behind-the-scenes footage and family vlogs. The channels have been so successful that Evan and his family have been able to turn their hobby into a full-time business. Today, EvanTubeHD has millions of subscribers and is one of the most popular toy review channels on YouTube. The family has also expanded their brand to include merchandise, such as t-shirts and toys, and has even published a book.

Business lessons from Evan's story:

1. **Capitalize on your interests:** Evan capitalized on his love for toys and games by creating a YouTube channel where he reviews them. Entrepreneurs should consider starting a business based on their interests or hobbies as it can help fuel their passion and make work more enjoyable.

2. **Collaborate with others:** Evan started his YouTube channel with the help of his father. Entrepreneurs should consider collaborating with others to bring new ideas and skills to their business.

3. **Consistency is key:** Evan has consistently uploaded videos to his YouTube channel over the years, building a loyal audience. Entrepreneurs should focus on consistency in their business, whether it be delivering quality products or services or maintaining a consistent brand image.

4. **Listen to your audience:** Evan takes feedback and requests from his audience, tailoring his content to their interests. Entrepreneurs should listen to their customers and make changes to their business based on their feedback.

5. **Embrace new opportunities:** Evan has expanded his business beyond YouTube, selling his own merchandise and partnering with other companies. Entrepreneurs should be open to new opportunities and be willing to adapt and evolve their business over time.

Exercise: Marketing Avengers

In this exercise, you will learn how to create a marketing plan by identifying your target audience, defining your unique selling proposition, setting marketing goals, developing marketing strategies, and creating an action plan to implement those strategies.

1: Identifying the Target Audience
- Who are the people we want to reach with our product or service?
- What are their needs, interests, and behaviors?
- How can we reach them in the most effective way?

2: Defining the Unique Selling Proposition
- What makes our product or service different from others?
- How can we communicate our unique features to the target audience?
- Why should people choose our product or service over others?

3: Setting Marketing Goals
- What do we want to achieve with our marketing efforts?
- How can we measure the success of our marketing campaign?
- What resources do we need to achieve our marketing goals?

4: Developing Marketing Strategies
- What are the different marketing channels we can use to reach our target audience?
- How can we create engaging content that appeals to our target audience?
- What promotions or incentives can we offer to encourage people to try our product or service?

5: Creating an Action Plan

- What specific steps do we need to take to implement our marketing strategies?
- Who will be responsible for each step?
- When will each step be completed?

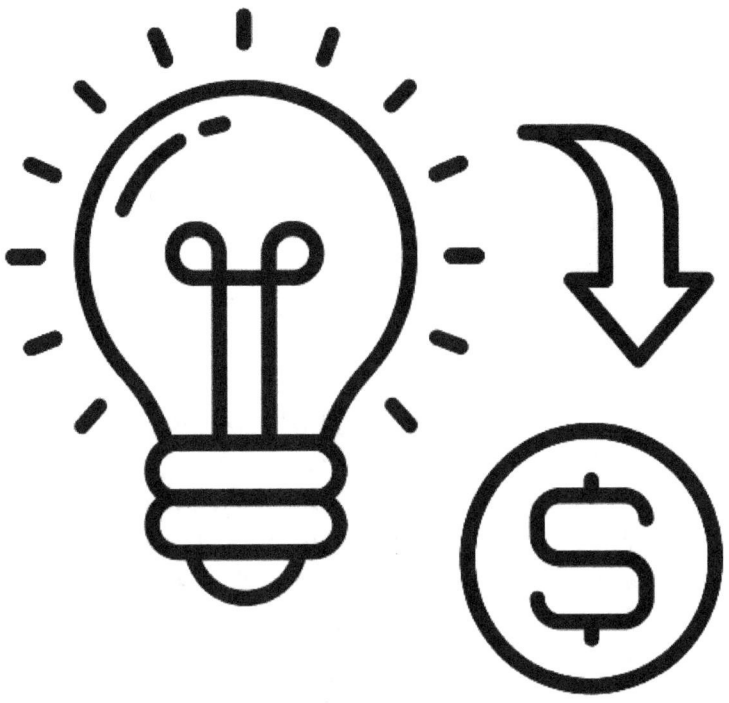

Chapter 6: Making money

Making money is an important part of running a business. Here are some things you can do to make sure your business is successful and profitable:

1. **Price your products or services correctly.** Make sure you're charging enough to cover your expenses and make a profit. Research what other businesses in your industry are charging and make sure your prices are competitive.
2. **Keep your expenses low.** Look for ways to save money on things like supplies, equipment, and marketing materials. Be smart about how you spend your money and always look for ways to cut costs.
3. **Find new customers.** The more customers you have, the more money you can make! Look for ways to reach new customers, like participating in community events or using social media to promote your business.
4. **Offer great customer service.** Happy customers are more likely to come back and refer their friends and family to your business. Make sure you're offering excellent customer service and always going above and beyond to make your customers happy.

With hard work and determination, you can create a successful and profitable business.

Making Profit and Being Frugal

1. How can you make sure you're charging enough for your products or services to cover your expenses and make a profit?
2. What are some ways you can keep your business expenses low, like saving money on supplies or equipment?
3. How can you reach new customers and expand your customer base, such as by participating in community events or using social media to promote your business?
4. Why is offering great customer service important for your business, and how can you make sure you're always going above and beyond to make your customers happy?

How can we price our products or services?

Pricing your products or services can be tricky, but here are some tips to help you get started:

1. **Know your costs.** Make sure you know how much it costs to produce your product or service. This includes things like supplies, equipment, and labor. Once you know your costs, you can set a price that will allow you to make a profit.
2. **Research your competition.** Look at what other businesses in your industry are charging for similar products or services. This will give you an idea of what people are willing to pay and help you set a competitive price.
3. **Consider your target market.** Think about who your customers are and how much they're willing to pay for your product or service. If you're targeting a high-end market, you may be able to charge more than if you're targeting a budget-conscious market.
4. **Experiment with pricing.** Don't be afraid to experiment with different prices to see what works best for your business. You may find that you can charge more than you thought, or that you need to lower your prices to attract more customers.

Pricing your products or services is all about finding a balance between making a profit and being competitive. Be sure to factor in your costs, research your competition, and consider your target market when setting your prices.

How will you price?

1. What are some things that you need to consider when setting a price for your product or service?
2. How can you find out what your competition is charging for similar products or services?
3. Why is it important to think about your target market when setting a price?
4. What can you do if you find that your pricing isn't working well for your business?

How can we make sure we're making money?

How can we make sure we're making more money than we're spending? It's important to keep track of your finances to make sure you're making a profit. Here are some tips to help you stay on top of your finances:

Create a budget. A budget is a plan for how you will spend your money. Make sure you're accounting for all of your expenses, including supplies, equipment, and marketing materials. Then, compare your expenses to your income to make sure you're making more money than you're spending.

Track your income and expenses. Keep a record of all the money coming in and going out of your business. This will help you identify areas where you may be overspending or where you could be making more money.

Look for ways to cut costs. Be smart about how you spend your money and look for ways to cut costs. This could include things like buying supplies in bulk, using cheaper materials, or finding more affordable marketing strategies.

Set financial goals. Decide how much money you want to make in a certain amount of time, and create a plan for how you will achieve your goals. This will help you stay motivated and focused on making a profit.

Making a profit takes time and effort. It's important to be patient and stay focused on your goals. But with hard work and determination, you can create a successful and profitable business that makes a positive impact on the world around you.

Budget Smart

1. What is a budget and why is it important for a business?
2. How can you keep track of your income and expenses?
3. What are some ways to cut costs for your business?
4. Why is it important to set financial goals for your business?

Ideas in Action: Financial Planning

In this section, which I call "Ideas in Action," we will explore how theories can be put into practice by using the classic example of a lemonade stand business.

Financial plan for a lemonade stand, including some exemplary numbers and amounts:

- **Income:** Let's say the lemonade stand sells 50 cups of lemonade per day at $1 per cup, for a daily income of $50.
- **Cost of goods sold:** Each cup of lemonade costs $0.25 to make (for lemons, sugar, water, and cups), for a total daily cost of $12.50.
- **Gross profit: The** lemonade stand's gross profit per day is $37.50 ($50 - $12.50).
- **Overhead expenses:** There may be additional expenses, such as a cost of the stand, signage, or other supplies. Let's say these expenses add up to $5 per day.
- **Net profit:** After overhead expenses, the lemonade stand's net profit per day is $32.50 ($37.50 - $5).
- **Savings goal:** Let's say the lemonade stand owner wants to save up for a new bike that costs $100. If they save all of their net profit ($32.50) each day, they will reach their savings goal in just over 3 days ($100 / $32.50 = 3.08 days).

Case Study: Farrhad Acidwalla

Farrhad Acidwalla is an Indian entrepreneur who started his first company, Rockstah Media, at the age of 16. The company specialized in web design and development, and quickly gained a reputation for producing high-quality work.

Acidwalla's success with Rockstah Media led him to start several other ventures, including CYBERNETIV, a company that provided cybersecurity services, and Cipher 256, a digital marketing agency.

In addition to his entrepreneurial pursuits, Acidwalla is also a speaker and philanthropist. He has given talks at various conferences and events, and has donated a portion of his earnings to various charitable causes, including education and healthcare initiatives.

Despite his success, Acidwalla faced some setbacks along the way. He was arrested in 2012 on charges of cybercrime and fraud, which he maintained were unfounded. However, he was eventually cleared of all charges and continued to pursue his entrepreneurial endeavors.

Today, Acidwalla is considered one of the most successful young entrepreneurs in India.

Business lessons from Farrhad Acidwalla's story:

1. **Start early:** Farrhad Acidwalla started his first company at just 16 years old, showcasing that age is not a barrier to entrepreneurship. Entrepreneurs should start early and gain experience and skills to help them succeed in the business world.

2. **Build a strong team:** Acidwalla built a strong team of talented individuals to help him grow his businesses. Entrepreneurs should focus on building a strong team of employees who share their vision and can help them achieve their goals.

3. **Be innovative:** Acidwalla was innovative in his businesses, creating new and unique solutions to problems. Entrepreneurs should strive to be innovative and create new products or services that differentiate them from competitors.

4. **Take calculated risks:** Acidwalla took calculated risks in his business, such as expanding to new markets and investing in new ventures. Entrepreneurs should be willing to take risks in their business, but also evaluate the potential risks and rewards before making a decision.

5. **Learn from failures:** Acidwalla experienced failures in his businesses, such as with the closure of his social media agency. However, he used these failures as learning opportunities and used the experience to improve his future businesses. Entrepreneurs should learn from their failures and use them to improve their future endeavors.

Exercise: "Let's Make a Budget!"

Introduction: Starting a new business can be exciting, but it's important to plan carefully to make sure you have enough money to cover your expenses. In this exercise, you'll learn how to make a budget for your new business.

Steps:

1. **List your expenses:** Think about all the things you'll need to pay for to start your business. Some examples might include:

- Rent for a storefront or office space
- Equipment and supplies
- Inventory
- Marketing and advertising
- Insurance and permits
- Utilities and other bills

2. **Estimate your income:** How much money do you think you'll make from selling your products or services? Be realistic and do some research to find out what similar businesses are charging.

3. **Subtract your expenses from your income:** Once you have a list of your expenses and an estimate of your income, subtract your expenses from your income to see if you're making a profit. If your expenses are higher than your income, you may need to make some adjustments to your budget.

4. **Look for ways to cut costs:** If your expenses are higher than your income, think about ways you can reduce your costs. For example, you could find a cheaper storefront or office space, buy used equipment instead of new, or do your own marketing and advertising.

5. **Revise and update your budget regularly:** Your budget isn't set in stone, so make sure to revisit it regularly and make adjustments as needed. As your business grows and changes, your expenses and income may change as well.

Chapter 7: Growing our business

Growing our business is an exciting part of being an entrepreneur. Here are some tips to help you grow your business:

1. **Expand your product or service line.** Look for ways to add new products or services that complement what you're already offering. This will give your customers more options and help you reach new markets.
2. **Increase your marketing efforts.** Look for new ways to promote your business, like using social media, offering special promotions or deals, or attending industry events.
3. **Hire employees or outsource tasks.** If you're feeling overwhelmed or need help with certain tasks, consider hiring employees or outsourcing some of your work. This will allow you to focus on the aspects of your business that you enjoy and are best at.
4. **Expand to new markets.** Look for opportunities to expand your business to new markets, either by opening a new location or by selling your products or services online.

New Products, New Markets

1. What are some ways you can add new products or services to your business?
2. What are some ways you can expand your business to new markets?
3. Why might it be helpful to hire employees or outsource some tasks for your business? Who could be your new employees or partners?
4. Who could bring new and big customer?

How can we keep improving what we offer?

Continuously improving what you offer is essential to running a successful business. Here are some tips to help you keep improving:

1. **Listen to your customers.** Your customers are the best source of feedback on your products or services. Ask them for their opinions, and use their feedback to improve what you offer.
2. **Keep up with industry trends.** Stay up-to-date on what's happening in your industry and what your competitors are doing. This will help you identify areas where you can improve and stay ahead of the competition.
3. **Experiment with new ideas.** Don't be afraid to try new things and take risks. Experiment with new products or services, marketing strategies, or business models to see what works best for your business.
4. **Continuously learn and grow.** Read books, attend workshops, or take courses to learn new skills and ideas. This will help you stay motivated and inspired to keep improving.

Continuously improving what you offer is an exciting part of your journey. Enjoy the process and be open to learning and trying new things along the way.

Learning from your customers and business

1. How can we get feedback from our customers about our products or services?
2. Why is it important to keep up with industry trends and what our competitors are doing?
3. What are some ways we can experiment with new ideas for our business?
4. Why is it important to continuously learn and grow as entrepreneurs?

Ideas in Action: Growing your Business

In this section, which I call "Ideas in Action," we will explore how theories can be put into practice by using the classic example of a lemonade stand business.

Let's think about how we can grow our lemonade business.

1. Add new products or services to your stand, like snacks or healthy options, to attract more customers and give them more options to choose from.
2. Get creative with your marketing! Try making posters or flyers, or even creating a social media page for your business. You could also offer special deals or promotions to attract new customers.
3. Consider hiring friends or family members to help out with the stand, or outsource some tasks to a local business to reduce the workload and stress.
4. Think about expanding your business to new markets. Maybe you could open a second stand next to a bus stop or another busy location or start selling your lemonade online to reach customers who can't visit your stand in person. These strategies will help you grow your lemonade stand business and make it even more successful!

Case Study: Adam Horwitz

Adam Horwitz is an American entrepreneur who started his first business when he was just 15 years old. He created a website called UrbanGeekz that focused on technology news and trends for urban audiences.

Horwitz's success with UrbanGeekz led him to start several other ventures, including mobile app development companies and social media marketing agencies. He also wrote a book called "Mobile Monopoly", which detailed his journey as a young entrepreneur and offered advice to others looking to start their own businesses.

Horwitz's success was not without its challenges, however. He faced criticism from those who believed he was too young to be taken seriously as a business owner. Nevertheless, he persevered and continued to build his businesses.

Today, Horwitz is considered one of the most successful young entrepreneurs in the United States. He has been featured in several media outlets, including Forbes and The Huffington Post, and has inspired countless others to pursue their entrepreneurial dreams.

Business lessons from Adam Horwitz's story:

1. **Identify opportunities:** Adam Horwitz identified a need for technology news and trends focused on urban audiences, which led him to start UrbanGeekz. Entrepreneurs should identify a specific niche or target audience to serve, as it can help differentiate their business from competitors.

2. **Stay focused on your goals:** Horwitz remained focused on his goal of creating a successful business, despite facing challenges and setbacks. Entrepreneurs should stay focused on their goals and remain motivated to overcome obstacles and achieve success.

3. **Embrace new technologies:** Horwitz embraced new technologies and used them to his advantage in his businesses, such as mobile app development and social media marketing. Entrepreneurs should stay up-to-date with new technologies and use them to improve their businesses.

4. **Build a strong brand:** Horwitz built a strong brand with UrbanGeekz, which helped him attract a loyal audience. Entrepreneurs should focus on building a strong brand identity and maintaining consistency in their branding.

5. **Collaborate with others:** Horwitz collaborated with other entrepreneurs and businesses, such as through joint ventures and partnerships. Entrepreneurs should consider collaborating with others to bring new ideas and skills to their business.

Exercise: Grow Your Business

Introduction: Do you have a business that you want to make even better? In this exercise, you'll learn how to grow your business by attracting new customers, improving your products or services, and increasing your revenue.

Step 1: Identify Your Target Customers

- Who are your target customers?
- What are their needs and wants?
- How can you reach them effectively?

Step 2: Offer Something New

- What new product or service can you offer to attract more customers?
- How can you make it unique and different from what others are offering?
- How much will it cost to offer this new product or service?

Step 3: Expand Your Reach

- What new channels can you use to reach your target customers?
- How can you use social media, email marketing, or other platforms to connect with them?
- What partnerships or collaborations can you establish to reach new audiences?

Step 4: Improve Customer Experience

- How can you make your customers happier and more satisfied?
- What improvements can you make to your products or services?
- How can you make the customer experience better?

Step 5: Measure and Optimize

- How can you measure the success of your growth hacks?
- What metrics should you track to evaluate your progress?
- How can you optimize your strategies to continue growing your business?

Chapter 8: Let's learn how to handle challenges!

Let's learn **how to handle challenges!** Running a business is not always easy, and you will likely face challenges along the way. Here are some tips to help you handle challenges:

1. **Stay positive.** Maintaining a positive attitude is key to overcoming challenges. Believe in yourself and your ability to find solutions to problems.
2. **Keep your eyes on the target.** When faced with a challenge, it's important to stay focused on your goals and stay motivated to keep moving forward.
3. **Look for solutions.** When you encounter a challenge, don't get discouraged. Instead, look for solutions and brainstorm ways to overcome the challenge.
4. **Learn from your mistakes.** Every challenge is an opportunity to learn and grow. Use your challenges as a chance to reflect on what you can do better next time.

Resilience is the ability to keep going and not give up, even when things are tough or don't go as planned. It's like being a superhero, because you can bounce back and keep trying until you reach your goals. Resilience is important because it helps us face challenges and learn from our mistakes.

Jump Over Hurdles

1. How can a positive attitude help you overcome challenges in your business?
2. Why is it important to stay focused on your goals when facing a challenge?
3. How can you brainstorm solutions to overcome a challenge in your business?
4. What can you learn from your mistakes and challenges, and how can you use that knowledge to improve your business?

What should we do when things don't go as planned?

What should we do when things don't go as planned? Even with the best intentions and planning, sometimes things don't go as expected. Here are some tips to help you handle these situations:

1. **Stay calm.** When things don't go as planned, it's easy to get upset or frustrated. Instead, take a deep breath and try to stay calm.
2. **Evaluate the situation.** Take a step back and evaluate the situation. What went wrong, and what can you do to fix it?
3. **Look for solutions.** Brainstorm ways to solve the problem and come up with a plan of action.
4. **Ask for help.** Don't be afraid to ask for help or advice from others. Sometimes a fresh perspective can help you see things in a new light.

Calm Down and Adapt

1. How can we stay calm when things don't go as planned?
2. What steps can we take to evaluate the situation?
3. How can we brainstorm solutions to solve the problem?
4. When is it okay to ask for help and advice from others?

How can we keep going when things get tough?

Running a business can be challenging, and there may be times when you feel discouraged or overwhelmed. Here are three tips to help you keep going:

1. **Focus on the half-full glass:** When things get tough, it's easy to focus on the negative. Instead, try to focus on the positive things that are happening in your business. Maybe you made a new sale or received positive feedback from a customer. By focusing on the positive, you can stay motivated and inspired to keep going.

2. **Take a break:** Sometimes when things get tough, it's important to take a step back and give yourself time to rest and recharge. Take a break and do something that you enjoy, like spending time with friends or family, exercising, or reading a book. This will help you come back to your work with renewed energy and focus.

3. **Change your perspective:** When things get tough, it's easy to get stuck in a negative mindset. Instead, try to shift your perspective and look at the situation from a different angle. Ask yourself, "What can I learn from this?" or "How can I use this experience to grow and improve?" By changing your perspective, you can turn a negative experience into a positive opportunity.

With hard work and perseverance, you can overcome any challenge that comes your way.

Perspective is everything

1. What are some activities we can do to take a break and recharge when we're feeling overwhelmed?
2. How can changing our perspective help us turn a negative experience into a positive opportunity?
3. Why is it important to shift our focus away from negative thoughts when facing challenges in our business?

Ideas in Action: Handling Challenges
Be adaptable and flexible:

Let's say you have a lemonade stand and it's a really hot day, but suddenly it starts to rain.

1. You might feel sad and frustrated because you were hoping to make a lot of money selling lemonade. But if you're adaptable and flexible, you can think of a new plan.
2. Find a new solution: Maybe you can move your stand under a tree or umbrella to keep dry, or you can offer to deliver lemonade to people's homes instead.
3. Don't give up: Even though the rain was a challenge, you didn't give up and found a new way to keep your business going.

This is why it's important to be adaptable and flexible – it helps you find new solutions to problems and keep moving forward.

Case Study: Maddie Bradshaw

Maddie Bradshaw is an American entrepreneur who started her own jewelry company, M3 Girl Designs, when she was just 10 years old. The company initially sold bottle cap jewelry, which Bradshaw created by hand using recycled bottle caps.

M3 Girl Designs quickly gained popularity, and Bradshaw began selling her jewelry at local markets and online. As the company grew, she expanded her product line to include other types of jewelry, as well as accessories and clothing.

Bradshaw's success with M3 Girl Designs led her to start several other ventures, including a line of scented jewelry and a mobile app development company. She has also written a book called "Maddie Bradshaw's You Can Start a Business, Too!", which offers advice to other young people looking to start their own businesses.

Despite her success, Bradshaw remains humble and focused on giving back. She has donated a portion of her earnings to various charitable causes, including education and healthcare initiatives.

Business lessons from Maddie Bradshaw's story:

1. **Identify a need:** Maddie Bradshaw identified a need for unique and personalized accessories for tween girls, which led her to start her business, M3 Girl Designs. Entrepreneurs should identify a specific need or problem to solve, as it can help differentiate their business from competitors.

2. **Be creative:** Bradshaw used her creativity to design unique and personalized accessories, which helped her stand out in the market. Entrepreneurs should be creative in their business to create products or services that are distinctive and memorable.

3. **Listen to your customers:** Bradshaw took customer feedback into account when designing her products, which helped her meet their specific needs and desires. Entrepreneurs should listen to their customers and make changes to their business based on their feedback.

4. **Focus on quality:** Bradshaw's products were high-quality and unique, which helped her build a loyal customer base. Entrepreneurs should focus on providing quality products or services to their customers in order to build a strong reputation and customer loyalty.

5. **Collaborate with others:** Bradshaw collaborated with other businesses and designers, which helped her expand her product line and reach new customers. Entrepreneurs should consider collaborating with others to bring new ideas and skills to their business.

Exercise: Solving Business Problems

Introduction: In business, problems are inevitable, but we can learn to solve them with creativity and strategy.

1. **Identify the problem:** What is the issue that needs to be addressed?
2. **Brainstorm solutions:** Think of as many solutions as possible, even if they seem unconventional or unrealistic.
3. **Evaluate the options:** Consider the pros and cons of each solution, and determine which ones are the most feasible and effective.
4. **Implement the solution:** Once a solution has been chosen, create an action plan with specific steps to carry out the solution and assign responsibilities to team members if necessary.

Solving Business Problems Template:

Problem Description:

Possible solutions:
Solution A

Solution B

Solution C

Evaluation and Comparison of Solutions:

Preferred Solution:

Action Plan:
Step 1:
Responsible person:
Deadline:

Step 2:
Responsible person:
Deadline:

Step 3:
Responsible person:
Deadline:

Step 4:
Responsible person:
Deadline:

Conclusion

Congratulations on finishing this book! By reading this book, you have taken the first step towards becoming an entrepreneur. You now have a better understanding of what it means to be an entrepreneur and how you can turn your passions and ideas into a successful business.

In Chapter 1, we explored the concept of entrepreneurship and why it is cool to be an entrepreneur. We learned that being an entrepreneur means taking risks and creating something new. We also learned that being an entrepreneur can be a lot of fun!

Chapter 2 was all about finding your passion. We discussed how important it is to identify your strengths and passions to find a business idea that you are truly passionate about. When you do something you love, you are more likely to succeed.

In Chapter 3, we learned about idea generation. We brainstormed ways to solve problems in our community and turn our ideas into something real. We learned that it's important to be creative and think outside the box when it comes to business ideas.

Chapter 4 was all about business planning. We learned how to identify our customers, calculate our start-up costs, and set financial goals for our business. We also learned how to create a budget and track our expenses.

In Chapter 5, we explored different ways to spread the word about our business. We learned how to create eye-catching displays, use social media, and offer discounts or incentives to get people excited about our business.

Chapter 6 focused on making money. We learned how to price our products or services and make sure we're making more money than we're spending. We also learned the importance of keeping our expenses low and finding new customers.

In Chapter 7, we learned how to grow our business. We explored ways to expand our product or service line, increase our marketing efforts, and hire employees or outsource tasks.

Finally, in Chapter 8, we learned how to handle challenges. We discussed the importance of staying positive, evaluating the situation, looking for solutions, and asking for help.

By reading this book, you now have a better understanding of what it takes to start and run a successful business. Remember, being an entrepreneur takes hard work, dedication, and a willingness to take risks. But with the right mindset and a passion for what you do, you can achieve anything you set your mind to. So go out there and start your own business!

Acknowledgement

I would like to express my gratitude to my parents, who were my biggest supporters throughout my journey as an entrepreneur. It all started back in elementary school with a small bookstand, and their unwavering encouragement and guidance helped me to grow and develop my entrepreneurial spirit. Even though they are no longer with me, I will always cherish the memories of their belief in me, which gave me the confidence to pursue my dreams.